101

Uses *for* *an* **Old**

Harley

Voyageur Press

A TOWN SQUARE BOOK

Text © 2003 by Voyageur Press, Inc.
Photography © 2003 by sources as noted

Edited by Amy Rost-Holtz
Designed by Maria Friedrich
Printed in China

03 04 05 06 07 5 4 3 2 1

Library of Congress Cataloging-in-Publication Data available

ISBN 0-89658-035-0

Distributed in Canada by Raincoast Books, 9050 Shaughnessy Street, Vancouver, B.C. V6P 6E5

Published by Voyageur Press, Inc.
123 North Second Street, P.O. Box 338, Stillwater, MN 55082 U.S.A.
651-430-2210, fax 651-430-2211
books@voyageurpress.com
www.voyageurpress.com

Endpapers: Harley-Davidson enthusiasts line up to show off their mounts in the 1930s.

Front cover: Photograph © Keith Baum/ BaumsAway! Stock Photography; motorcycle courtesy of Motor City Harley-Davidson

Frontis: Photograph © Jerry Irwin

Title page: Dad, Mom, and Baby take the family Harley and sidecar out for spin during a Fourth of July celebration.

Facing page, left: A young Harley fan, all dressed up and ready to ride

Facing page, right: A classic 1950s Harley-Davidson ad

Acknowledgments

Thanks to those who helped bring this book to life, including Keith Baum, Jerry Irwin, Pamela Percy, and the staff at Voyageur Press.

1

New beginnings

Outside an early dealership in New England, more than a dozen new Harley-Davidsons stand all boxed up and ready to go out to their new homes.

2
Limousine

The owner of this early Harley-Davidson found more status in being chauffered around in the sidecar than riding the motor-cycle himself.

3

Santa's sleigh

Who needs eight tiny reindeer when you've got a Big Twin?
(Photograph © Jerry Irwin)

4

Mardi Gras float

A Harley-Davidson owner shows off a flair with feathers and a passion for purple at the annual Sturgis Motorcycle Rally. (Photograph © Jerry Irwin)

5

Beach bum

A rider and his Harley-Davidson Silent Gray Fellow share a peaceful moment contemplating the waves. Even in their earliest versions, Harley-Davidson motorcycles were seen by many as a means of escape.

6

Dune buggy

A bathing beauty and her companion take their Harley-Davidson sidecar outfit for a spin in the sand and surf.

7
Pot of gold

A Harley-Davidson awaits the lucky leprechaun at the end of a rainbow.

8

Pretty in pink

This pink Softail is accessorized with white saddlebags and plenty of fringe. (Photograph © Keith Baum/BaumsAway! Stock Photography)

9

Posse

The Butte, Montana, Motorcycle Club shows off its Harley-Davidsons and other early motorcycles in 1914.

10

Dock

Two riders take their Harley-Davidson on a lakeside outing in 1921.

11
Fishing boat

Arthur Davidson, one of the founders of Harley-Davidson, and his friend display their catches during a 1916 fishing trip.

12

Big game trophy

Dressed in buffalo hide, this "Bison-Glide" Harley-Davidson should be right at home as it crosses the South Dakota prairie on its way to Sturgis. (Photograph © Keith Baum/BaumsAway! Stock Photography)

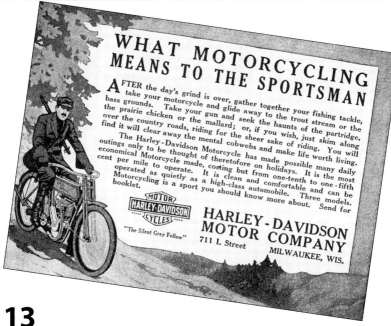

WHAT MOTORCYCLING MEANS TO THE SPORTSMAN

AFTER the day's grind is over, gather together your fishing tackle, take your motorcycle and glide away to the trout stream or the bass grounds. Take your gun and seek the haunts of the partridge, the prairie chicken or the mallard; or, if you wish, just skim along over the country roads, riding for the sheer sake of riding. You will find it will clear away the mental cobwebs and make life worth living.

The Harley-Davidson Motorcycle has made possible many daily outings only to be thought of theretofore on holidays. It is the most economical Motorcycle made, costing but from one-tenth to one-fifth cent per mile to operate. It is clean and comfortable and can be operated as quietly as a high-class automobile. Three models. Motorcycling is a sport you should know more about. Send for booklet.

HARLEY-DAVIDSON
MOTOR CYCLES
TRADE MARK

"The Silent Gray Fellow"

HARLEY-DAVIDSON MOTOR COMPANY
711 L Street
MILWAUKEE, WIS.

13

Hunting buddy

Although it's hard to imagine today's sleek, stylish Harleys crashing through the undergrowth after a partridge or mallard, early ads proclaimed the motorcycles to be a sportsman's best friend.

14
Sport utility vehicle

A colorful advertisement promotes the Harley as the sport utility vehicle of the 1930s.

HARLEY-DAVIDSON *for* 1930

15

Mountain climber

In the 1920s and 1930s, Harley-Davidson–style motorcycling was depicted as a rugged, outdoors, off-road activity.

16
Ego booster

In 1915, Charles F. Barrett won the Utica, New York, Auto Club hillclimb race on a Harley-Davidson single-cylinder.

This ad claimed the new world's record "came as a complete surprise" to the Harley-Davidson company, but it was still a cause for celebration, as well as promotion.

A New World's Record

Ray Watkins and Ben Torres Ride 346 Miles in 7 hours on a dirt track with an 8 H.P. Harley-Davidson

AT San Jose, Cal., December 8th, the regular stock eight horse power Harley-Davidson established a new world's record by covering 346 miles in seven hours.

The winning Harley-Davidson team finished 17 miles ahead of their nearest competitor and more than 12 miles ahead of the former world's record, although it was made on a board track. In addition to winning the first prize the Harley-Davidson also made the fastest mile in the contest.

During the whole run not a single repair, replacement or even adjustment was made to the Harley-Davidson and not a stop of any nature whatsoever was made except for change of riders and to take on gasoline and oil.

RAY WATKINS   BEN TORRES

As manufacturers we do not support racing and do not build racing machines. This new record came as a complete surprise to us. The contest was conducted entirely without our knowledge and the first we heard of it was a newspaper clipping sent in to the factory.

We have repeatedly asserted that the eight horse power Harley-Davidson was the fastest stock machine made, barring none. This has been proved time and again in contests where private owners competed with their own machines. This San Jose victory furnishes more actual proof that the Harley-Davidson will stand up under the most trying conditions possible and at a maintained high speed. The Harley-Davidson averaged 49.43 miles per hour for the entire 7 hours, including all stops for gas and oil.

The San Jose contest was conducted under F. A. M. sanction.

Harley-Davidson Motor Company

Producers of High-Grade Motorcycles for Eleven Years

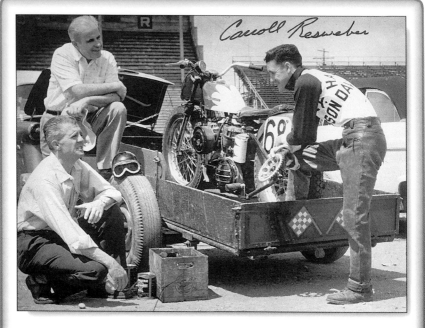

Carroll Resweber

18

Conversation piece

Carroll Resweber (right) was one of Harley-Davidson's top race riders in the 1950s.

19

Crowd pleaser

An echelon of Harley riders assembled at Daytona Beach in the 1950s.

20
Trampoline

Ads promised that fun-loving kids would jump at the chance to meet the new Harley-Davidson Topper motorscooter of the 1960s.

New! A Scooter by

HARLEY-DAVIDSON

Tops them all in beauty and performance

...it's the *Topper*

Fun-loving Jacks (and Jills, too) are jumping at the chance to meet the new Harley-Davidson Topper. And why not? There's not another motor scooter like it — combining clean, smart beauty with the newest mechanical secrets of success. Scootaway automatic transmission makes handling a dream . . . lowest center of gravity makes handling a dream . . See the new Topper at your Harley-Davidson dealer. Or write for free, colorful folder.

HARLEY-DAVIDSON MOTOR CO.
Milwaukee 1, Wisconsin, Dept. P
World's leading manufacturer of lightweight motor vehicles

21

Balance beam

Steady balance and strong bungee cords were the keys to leading the local Fourth of July parade from atop a Harley.

22

Jungle gym

Eight Chicago police officers form a moving human-Harley sculpture during a trick-riding practice in the 1920s. (Chicago Daily News negatives collection, DN-0089276. Courtesy of the Chicago Historical Society)

SOLOS

SERVI-CARS

23
Tricycle

24
Ice cream truck

Introduced in 1932, the three-wheel Harley-Davidson Servi-Car was used as a delivery vehicle by the U.S. Postal Service, police departments, the military, and private companies.

25
Diner

A Harley-Davidson doubles as a drive-in diner in this vintage soda pop ad.

26
Picnic basket

In the 1950s, Harley-Davidson bolstered its all-American reputation with publicity photos portraying the motorcycles as good, clean, wholesome fun.

27

Sunday drive

A Minnesota family takes their Harley twin and sidecar out for a leisurely afternoon on the road. (Minnesota Historical Society)

28
Tour bus

A 1930 sales catalog encouraged people to visit "America the beautiful" on the back of a Harley-Davidson.

29

Road trip

A 1939 ad promoted the Harley-Davidson as a convenient and economical means of travel.

30
Recreational vehicle

Designed for the ultimate in rider comfort during long hours and many miles on the road, some of today's Harleys are equipped with everything but a kitchen sink. (Photograph © Keith Baum/ BaumsAway! Stock Photography)

31
Room with a view

With no windows or roof to block the splendid view, a Harley is the ideal way to appreciate America's scenic sights. (Photograph © Jerry Irwin)

32

Scenic overlook

Sometimes the Harley itself is the main attraction. Here a group of riders take in a beautiful view of a Kucklehead. (Photograph © Jerry Irwin)

33
Shop teacher

Motorcycle racers often have to be their own mechanics. This racer wrenches on his WR at the Minnesota State Fair racetrack. (Michael Dregni collection)

34
Salvage yard

35
Thrift store

Anything and everything is an accouterment for this Harley, on display at the Daytona Motorcycle Rally in 2000. (Photograph © Jerry Irwin)

36
Stilts

Long forks make this Harley chopper stand tall and lay back.
(Photograph © Jerry Irwin)

37
Artist's canvas

A glorious marriage of painting and sculpture, this Harley-Davidson is covered with graphics, metal castings, and engravings. (Photograph © Jerry Irwin)

38

Salute

The tank on this Harley-Davidson makes a vibrant patriotic statement. (Photograph © Jerry Irwin)

39

Catwalk

As if they were on a fashion runway, riders strut their stuff on a narrow causeway lined with other high-style Harley-Davidsons. (Photograph © Jerry Irwin)

40

Tanning booth

Get a tan for your back on the back of your Harley. (Photograph © Jerry Irwin)

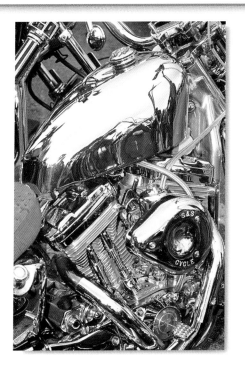

41
Mirror

The shiny chrome of this Harley custom reflects its owner's pride.
(Photograph © Jerry Irwin)

42

Hair dryer

"Somewhere on a desert highway, she rides a Harley-Davidson, her long, blonde hair flyin' in the wind…." —Neil Young, "Unknown Legend" (Photograph © Jerry Irwin)

For *the* Assistant Manager of the Farm—Your Boy

Now that the farm labor shortage has become so serious he will be called on to do more and more of the work.

The quickest, cheapest method of transportation —the Harley-Davidson Motorcycle—is a real necessity for him. If you want to save immeasurable labor and time that is now so valuable, buy him a

HARLEY-DAVIDSON
"For 16 Years The Master Mount"

When that extra sack of seed is wanted quickly, when the cattle break into the corn up the road a ways, when a plow share breaks, with every minute meaning lost dollars, the boy and his Harley-Davidson will be the most important team on the farm.

Delays, which formerly meant hours, now become mere incidents in the day's work—and then in the evening on Sundays when the boy wants the pleasures he has earned, the Harley-Davidson is always ready—the cheapest form of quick transportation possible.

Your dealer has some surprising facts on Harley-Davidson costs. Drop in and see him, or send for catalog.

Harley-Davidson Motor Co.
643-A Street,
Milwaukee, Wis.

Have you seen the new Harley-Davidson Bicycles?

50 to 75 miles per gallon of gasoline
800 to 1200 miles per gallon of cylinder oil
5000 to 8000 miles per set of tires

43
Farm truck

Early Harley-Davidson advertisements promoted the motorcycles as a practical, cost-efficient farm vehicle—perfect for "when that extra sack of seed is wanted quickly, when the cattle break into the corn up the road, when a plow share breaks."

44

Pet carrier

Two gentlemen load a pack of their best friends into their Harley-Davidson sidecar.

45
Bird perch

This macaw proves that Harley riders are nothing if not colorful.
(Photograph © Jerry Irwin)

46
Chicken coop

Any chicken can ride a motorcycle, but only the most pampered get their own twenty-eight-inch Fat Boy. (Photograph © Jessica Y. Kaminski)

47
Field hand

Many hands make the load light—especially when there's lots of horsepower involved. (Photograph © Jerry Irwin)

48

Pack mule

After loading his gear on the pillion seat, this Harley rider is ready to hit the road. (Photograph © Jerry Irwin)

ROY ROGERS
RIDES AGAIN
see story page 2

49

Faithful steed

Roy Rogers found a Harley-Davidson to be the next best thing to Trigger.

50

Chariot

A Harley custom fit for an emperor. (Photograph © Jerry Irwin)

51
King's throne

As soon as his first records went gold, Elvis Presley bought a Harley-Davidson. From then on, he continued to order the latest and greatest from Milwaukee almost annually.

52

Queen's throne

"Alice in Dairyland"—the annually elected spokeswoman for
Wisconsin agriculture—was squired around the 1951 Wisconsin
State Fair by a Harley-Davidson. (Wisconsin Historical Society,
image number WHi-2000)

53

Cause for rebellion

Marlon Brando played the quintessential misunderstood motorcyclist in *The Wild One*.

Lots of Eggs & Lots of Motorcycles –

Easter Greeting

But _____

Here is the "Best Chick" out.

HARLEY-DAVIDSON MOTORCYCLES

J. A. FOIZIE, Lee

54

Breakfast of champions

A humorous dealer postcard introduced the 1914 Harley-Davidson V-twin.

55
Training wheels

The look on this boy's face says it all. After clambering aboard a Model S 125, the world was a new place full of wonder—and there's no looking back.

56
Dream machines

Two youngsters research their future purchases at Karl's Cycles in Minneapolis, Minnesota, a landmark for local riders for decades. (Minnesota Historical Society)

57

Flame thrower

Firepower is the key on the dragstrip. (Photograph © Jerry Irwin)

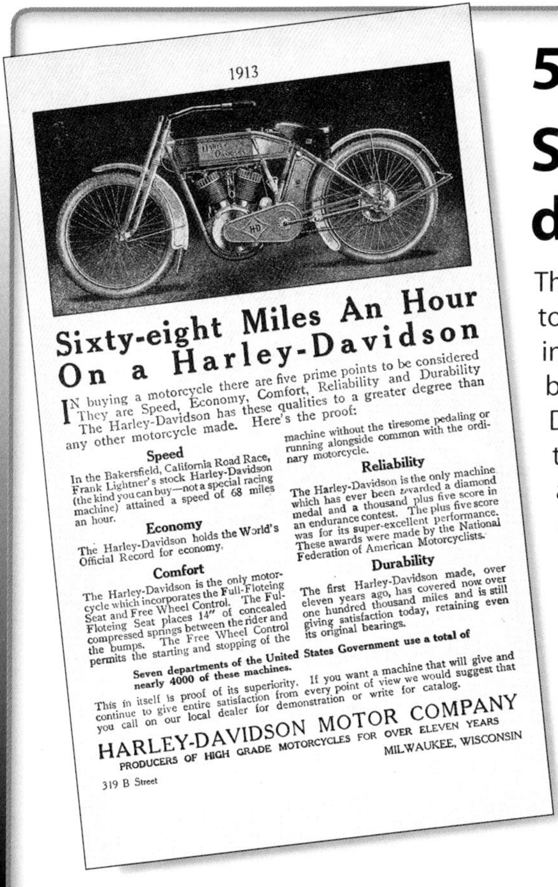
1913
Sixty-eight Miles An Hour
On a Harley-Davidson
IN buying a motorcycle there are five prime points to be considered They are Speed, Economy, Comfort, Reliability and Durability The Harley-Davidson has these qualities to a greater degree than any other motorcycle made. Here's the proof:
Speed
In the Bakersfield, California Road Race, Frank Lightner's stock Harley-Davidson (the kind you can buy—not a special racing machine) attained a speed of 68 miles an hour.
Economy
The Harley-Davidson holds the World's Official Record for economy.
Comfort
The Harley-Davidson is the only motorcycle which incorporates the Full-Floteing Seat and Free Wheel Control. The Ful-Floteing Seat places 14" of concealed compressed springs between the rider and the bumps. The Free Wheel Control permits the starting and stopping of the machine without the tiresome pedaling or running alongside common with the ordinary motorcycle.
Reliability
The Harley-Davidson is the only machine which has ever been awarded a diamond medal and a thousand plus five score in an endurance contest. The plus five score was for its super-excellent performance. These awards were made by the National Federation of American Motorcyclists.
Durability
The first Harley-Davidson made, over eleven years ago, has covered now over one hundred thousand miles and is still giving satisfaction today, retaining even its original bearings.
Seven departments of the United States Government use a total of nearly 4000 of these machines.
This in itself is proof of its superiority. If you want a machine that will give and continue to give entire satisfaction from every point of view we would suggest that you call on our local dealer for demonstration or write for catalog.
HARLEY-DAVIDSON MOTOR COMPANY
PRODUCERS OF HIGH GRADE MOTORCYCLES FOR OVER ELEVEN YEARS
MILWAUKEE, WISCONSIN
319 B Street

58

Speed demon

This 1913 ad is careful to note that this blistering speed was attained by a stock Harley-Davidson, "the kind that you can buy—not a special racing machine."

59
Rodeo clown

A nimble Harley cuts a tight corner during a barrel race.

60

Stunt double

Actor George Hamilton portrays the legendary Evel Knievel astride his trusty Harley-Davidson.

61
Thrill ride

A Harley-mounted rider "gets dizzy" circling a Wall of Death—a large, barrel-like chamber with high walls that form a vertical road. (Photograph © Jerry Irwin)

62

Show stopper

Don't try this at home! A combination tightrope-trapeze act proves to be an exercise in concentration and precision balance.

63

Leader of the pack

A group of happy Harley riders poses in formation at Daytona Beach in the 1950s.

64

Trusty sidekick

Police departments across the United States made use of the three-wheeled Harley-Davidson Servi-Car.

65
Chorus line

The motorcycle corps of the Minneapolis Police Department lines up its Harleys for a dignified department photo.

66
Sex symbol

A driver happily admires Jayne Mansfield's Harley-Davidson in this far-fetched publicity photo. (Library of Congress)

RALLY 'ROUND THE FUN WITH YOUNG AMERICA

67

Hot date

A 1960s ad promised that the Harley-Davidson Sportcycle would help riders get with "the in crowd."

68

Guy magnet

Dancer-actress Gertrude Hoffman attracts a flock of admirers with her Harley-Davidson motorcycle and sidecar.

69

Babe magnet

Girls love a guy on a Harley.

70

Girls' night out

Two country girls and their Harleys get ready to paint the town red.

71

Women's liberator

Easter Walters, a movie star and independent woman of the early 1900s, found freedom on a Harley-Davidson horizontal twin.

72

Honeymoon suite

A Harley-Davidson makes a romantic getaway vehicle in this advertisement. (Robert Jameson collection)

73
Couples therapy

The young couple spends some quality time together on their XLH.

74

Mother-daughter bonding

Maybe Mom would be a little more enthusiastic if she were the one steering the Harley.

75

Baby buggy

Sis dreams of the day when she's in the driver's seat, but for now must ride in style in the "baby buggy."

76

Family room

Nothing brings families together—in this case for a family portrait—like a Harley-Davidson.

77
Ice breaker

Wisconsin rider Oscar Bakke attached a runner to the front tire and chains to the back to make his Harley ice worthy. (Minnesota Historical Society)

TWICE ACROSS THE GREAT AMERICAN DESERT

I make my Expenses by Selling MY PHOTOGRAPHS
Price. What You Choose.

RICHARD E. NEW
Legless Motor Cycle Rider

78
Wheelchair

Legless motorcyclist Richard E. New crossed the country in a customized Harley-Davidson.

79

Getaway car

80

Easter basket

A well-dressed trio sits poised to make a clean getaway with a Harley and a wicker basket of a sidecar.

81

Bug zapper

Early Harleys were much more than just recreational road warriors. This Illinois mosquito abatement officer put his Harley to practical use hauling extermination equipment. (Chicago Daily News negatives collection, DN-0086754. Courtesy of the Chicago Historical Society)

82

Airplane

A police officer takes flight on a Harley during a practice for a police stunt show at Chicago's Soldier Field in the 1920s. (Chicago Daily News negatives collection, DN-0089272. Courtesy of the Chicago Historical Society)

83
Escort service

84
Air traffic control

Charles A. Lindbergh and his *Spirit of St. Louis* receive a Harley-Davidson escort upon arrival at a Chicago airfield. (Chicago Daily News negatives collection, DN-0084173. Courtesy of the Chicago Historical Society)

謹賀新年　一月元旦

85
Ambassador

A 1929 Japanese postcard shows Harley-Davidsons flanked by tanks.

86

Tank

A U.S. cavalry troop mounted on armored Harleys instead of horses assembled at Fort Brown, on the south Texas border, during the Mexican revolution, prior to World War I. (The Robert Runyon Photograph Collection [image number 00921], The Center for American History, The University of Texas at Austin)

87

Police lineup

A row of Harleys stand ready and waiting for the Philadelphia
Highway Patrol Drill Team. (Photograph © Keith Baum/
BaumsAway! Stock Photography)

88
Enforcer

No one escapes the long, two-wheeled arm of the law.

89

Christmas tree

A festive Harley lights up a snowy December night. (Photograph by Michael Dregni, motorcycle courtesy of Tom and Mona Theurer)

90

Diagram

Handy yellow arrows help riders put their parts in the right places.
(Photograph © Keith Baum/BaumsAway! Stock Photography;
motorcycle courtesy of Motor City Harley-Davidson)

91

Newscaster

In the 1920s, the *Chicago Daily News* was distributed to the city by Harley-riding delivery men nicknamed "Blue Streaks." (Chicago Daily News negatives collection, DN-0083660. Courtesy of the Chicago Historical Society)

92

Media event

William H. "Billy" Adams, governor of Colorado from 1927 to 1933, posed on a Harley-Davidson as part of promotional contest sponsored by a Denver Harley dealership and a local newspaper. (Photograph by Harry M. Rhoads, Denver Public Library, Western History Collection, RH-88)

93

Board room

Company executives (left to right) Gordon Davidson, William J. Harley, Arthur Davidson, and William H. Davidson convene to introduce the Harley-Davidson two-stroke motorcycle in 1948.

94
Executive power chair

Why claw your way to the top, when you could ride there in style?
And that way, you'll also have somewhere to sit when you arrive.

95

Time machine

An Amish buggy meets a Harley-Davidson by the side of country road in Pennsylvania. (Photograph © Jerry Irwin)

HARLEY-DAVIDSON DEAL

MAKES CLAIM OF RECORD

96
Missing link

The first Harley-Davidson, produced in 1903, transformed the bicycle into the motorcycle and introduced the world to a whole new form of transportation and recreation.

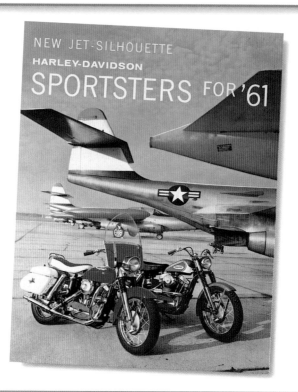

NEW JET-SILHOUETTE
HARLEY-DAVIDSON
SPORTSTERS FOR '61

97

The right stuff

The Harley-Davidson XLs had the right stuff in 1961.

98

Go cart

Motorcycles by definition have two wheels. That means this five-wheeled vehicle is another vehicle altogether, even though it still bears the Harley-Davidson moniker.

99
Lawn chair

A Harley twin makes for a fine place to rest after a long day.

100
Trophy case

There's no better place to set the trophy than on the gas tank of the faithful steed that won it.

101
Ride off into the sunset

This golden painting of an austere rider and his V-twin appeared in a 1913 issue of *The Harley-Davidson Dealer* magazine and was used in 1913 advertising posters.